AF227814

Little Good Things

Gratitude Affirmations (From a Cookie)

For Grandma Jean.

Text and illustrations by Eva Matheson.

This little book is just
for you...

Read it on hard days, happy days,
busy days, and quiet ones...

.

Come back to it whenever you
need a small reminder
that the little things
are often the biggest things of all.

Love, a little Cookie who's very glad you're here.

You're amazing
just the way you
are.

I'm lucky to
have you.

You make ordinary things feel special.

You're always kind.

I'll always choose you.
COOKIES

Thank you for being you.

Love is sharing the
last cookie.

You help me feel brave.

I'm a smart cookie...
Like you.

You deserve a world of happiness.

I love you more
than choc chips.

You want me
to dream big...

I want you
to dream
big too.

Life gets better
one cookie at a time.

I think
you're
brave and
strong.

If you're having a bad day...

Smile and
think
of me.

I'll be thinking of you too.

Choose kindness.
Choose cookies.

You make me laugh
when I feel sad.

You're my favourite kind of fun.

I doughnut
know what
I'd do
without you.

Everything about
you shines.

I love who you
are
not just what
you do.

I'm glad I've got you.

A balanced diet is
a cookie in each hand.

I believe in you.

You make hard things
look possible...

And that
makes me
belileve I can
do anything
too.

Thank you for being one
of life's little good things.

I'll always
need you.

I'll always look up to you.

Tough Cookie.
Someone with the right mixture
of sweetness and strength.

It's ok to fall down, sometimes I fall down too.

You are my safe place.

How did I
get so lucky?

Your dreams and
goals remind me that
mine matter too.

I'm proud of you.

. Life is better with you... and cookies.

You can't make everyone happy,
you're not a cookie.

Thank you for
everything you do.

You can never
be too sweet.

Kindness and Cookies
can fix almost anything.

You're simply the best.

You deserve
lots of hugs.

This Cookie Believes in You.

I'm fortunate to have you.

I followed my heart and
it led to cookies.

Your hugs warm me up.

I'm Cheering for you...

As loud as you cheer for me.

You are the best
part of my day.

You are my favourite.

I hope
you have the best day.

Happiness grows quietly
in the Little Good
Things.

Discover more books

https://eamatheson.com

www.ingramcontent.com/pod-product-compliance
Lightning Source LLC
Chambersburg PA
CBHW042050030726
47599CB00019B/2431

* 9 7 8 1 7 6 4 6 8 2 7 0 1 *